The Smart Series: Taking Smart Risks

The Smart Series: Taking Smart Risks

Another Great Book by
Award-Winning Author, Dr. Christine
Topjian

Authors Get Published

CONTENTS

CONTENTS

Published By: Authors Get Published
www.authorsgetpublished.com

First Printing, 2023

This book is dedicated to my dad, Dr. G. Topjian, who taught me when to take the right risks in life. I am always grateful for all you have taught me.

The Smart Series is a series of books written by Dr. Christine Topjian that teaches all about the smart ways. In life, if we wish to succeed, we have to do things the smart, educated, strategic way. The entire series is about the smart way to do everything.

This book is about the smart way to take risks. Because in life, there is always a risk.

Introduction

Fact: There are smart risks one can take in life and there are not so smart risks one can take in life.

When or if we engage in unintelligent risks, we are not doing ourselves any favors. Why? Because when we take non-intelligent risks, we are putting our valuable resources at-risk and we may lose our valuable resources.

How do we know where the smart, calculated risks are? How would we go about identifying them? How would we go about knowing where the right risks are and therefore, placing our money, our time, our resources on those right risks.

The answer comes down to looking, thinking, considering carefully and fully. And then of course, as with all of my books, there is a strong need to pray about it and to let God guide.

> If we don't read between the lines and we don't analyze things carefully, when we lose our resources, we have only ourselves to blame.

When I say looking carefully and analyzing something, I mean that we need to look very carefully at not only the information we are being presented with but the information that we are not being presented with but that can be inferred from the information given. What is written between the lines that is not being highlighted to us but is an ever-present factor and therefore, causes the entire schema to be a risky one? If we don't read between the lines and we don't analyze things carefully, when we lose our resources, we have only ourselves to blame.

Does that sound a bit harsh? I hope not. I say that because if we don't take the time to learn and to educate ourselves, then we have already lost the battle. I also say that because I have taken not so smart risks in the past and I have paid the price dearly but I have learned from my mistakes and this book is your call to learn from my mistakes, your mistakes and all the mistakes people around you have made. Because everyone makes mistakes and if we don't learn from our own and those of others, then we are not maximizing our learning and we will stand to keep making (sometimes the very same) mistakes.

Peppered throughout this book, you will find reflection questions (and some space provided for your responses) and you will find prayer suggestions. I have provided the reflection questions so that you can apply the concepts mentioned and taught to your own life (for your benefit) and the prayer suggestions because many people are not sure what words to use to pray. I have found good feedback from my readers who have said that they appreciate and enjoy the wording of my suggested prayers so that you can access your best life.

Chapter 10 of this book is all about how to be a sharp leader when the stakes are high and includes your 5 step guide on how to ensure you are operating at your highest when the stakes are high (and they always are).

One last note: you will really get much more out of this book if you read through the entire book, you really take the time to complete the reflection questions and you engage in the prayers. If we do not engage in prayer, we simply will not be activating the capabilities of God to operate and bring His best into our lives. If we are not activating His capabilities, then we are not operating at our best.

Let's get right into it then!

1

Read carefully

The first chapter of this book is going to dive right into my #1 point: you have to read everything carefully. Reading carefully helps you understand where you are placing your risk and where (if you have made a good decision) your reward will come from.

Anytime we are going to make an important step, we need to read everything we are presented with very carefully. It can be a very exciting time - we can be presented with a new offer to purchase a home, a new job or career opportunity, a new contract to buy or sell something, and the list goes on and on. And that is all great. But read everything. Read the fine print and ask questions. Find out what "they" may not be telling you, what they may not be sharing with you.

I remember being in a workshop one time and the instructor was advising us to do something not very up-front and honestly. When one of my fellow classmates asked the question "But wouldn't they find out?" the instructor's response was "They have too many applications to go through - do you really think they are going to check on yours!?"

Not the most honest fellow but some people, companies, organizations do think that way and unfortunately operate with less-than-honest information to their clients.

Sales and selling is all about putting the most attractive information up-front and in front of you so that you get really excited about the offer. It is the wise person who stops for a few moments and even though they are excited at a new opportunity, they have to make time to read everything and to consider everything. What may seem like a great opportunity when looked into more carefully may not be so or may be less so. It is really important to take the time to read everything carefully.

I recall very clearly a real estate deal I had in front of me. On the surface, everything looked ok. It looked like a standard agreement and people around me were getting excited. They were looking at it and seemed very pleased. And then I began to read more closely and began looking at the information in the Schedules (like the Addendums). Things stopped looking as good. We began to notice that little charges were added and certainly, had no part in the previous discussions we had engaged in with the other party.

Because I read more carefully, I made the best choice based on all the information that I now had.

> When you don't read everything carefully, things may seem great and you may get pretty excited.

When you don't read everything carefully, things may seem great and you may get pretty excited. I remember reading long ago that the way that most go is not always the best way and I have long held that belief. Just because many people are doing it, it doesn't mean it's the right thing for you or the best thing for you to do.

Can it be annoying and tedious to have to read all the details? Definitely. I get it. But once you have signed that contract, you are bound by its terms and conditions and that can get you into a whole heap of trouble if you aren't 100% of what you're signing.

Terms of Cancellation

Before taking on risk, take some time to read the terms of cancellation or how to opt-out should you choose to. You have to know how you can get out of a bad deal if you are in one and that needs to be figured out prior to signing on any dotted lines and passing over your payment.

2

Consider It Carefully

> Before you commit to something, consider all aspects of it carefully.

Before you commit to something, consider all aspects of it carefully. Consider whether this is a realistic commitment and consider whether there is purpose behind what you are doing. When there is no purpose behind something (your "why", if you will) then you are either not going to start or you are not going to stick to it, and something that you are not going to stick to is not going to be very helpful in the long run. Everything good takes time to accomplish so when we don't give it that time, guess what happens....it's not going to go very well.

Take a mortgage for example: if you are signing for a 10-year mortgage at a certain rate and with certain conditions, know that you are committing to that mortgage, the payments and the terms for many years. If you default, there will be consequences. If you make late payments, there will be consequences. If you wish to make pre-payments, there will be parameters and terms you will need to follow. I remember I was looking to make a pre-payment many years ago on a mortgage and checked with the banker about that. She reminded me that I was not eligible to put in that much into my mortgage pre-payment and that the maximum pre-payment amount in the mortgage would be exceeded with the amount I intended to put in. So, this meant that I was not able to put in that pre-payment amount and that I would not get that tax benefit for that year.

Bottom line: I hadn't read the fine print well enough and I would have had a financial setback if I had insisted on making that bigger payment.

The Role of Faith

Faith should play a tremendous role in your decision-making for any risk you take. I understand that some people may be a little nervous about this point but God will meet you where you are so ask Him to.

> I totally understand and get that some people are not firm believers or at least, are not sure if they should believe in or trust in God. I get it. When we don't have the benefit of years of experience with God or we didn't grow up with Him, we won't be sure of whether to trust in Him or not. But everybody has to start somewhere.

When we consider taking on risk for something (anything), we should really pray about it. We have to ask God what His take is on it because we are not able to see the full picture. God is. Now, I totally understand and get that some people are not firm believers or even, are not sure if they should believe in or trust in God. I get it. When we don't have the benefit of years of experience with God or we didn't grow up with that relationship with Him, we won't be sure of whether to trust in Him or not. But everybody has to start somewhere. So start with something small. Something easy. Something that doesn't require much trust at first. When I was first starting out, I started with something as simple as asking God to bring me something simple into my life and to see how that would work out. Then I asked Him to show me something that I didn't know about or wasn't sure existed. I then asked Him to explain something to me.

Dr. Virkler, the founder of Christian Leadership University, through which I did my first Doctorate and am doing my second, was a great affirmer of the truth for me. What truth is that? That God speaks to us, guides us, shows us how, when and where, makes promises to us and that in an effort to reach His best for us, we are to follow His guidance and His leadership through the indwelling Holy Spirit. I didn't know that much about God and Dr. Virkler's books, courses, resources and emails helped me to discover and to learn a little more about God's awesome personality.

One of the things that I learned is that God knows what is best for us (we don't) and that He knows the best and fastest way to get us to where we need to be. We may feel that something is taking a really long time but that is sometimes just because we may be a bit impatient because we are excited about it (I can get really excited about things I'm looking forward to). We need to trust in His timing and because this is a book about taking smart risks, we need to consult with God about which risks are the smart and right ones to undertake, and that very much includes the timing of the blessing(s).

Prayer Suggestion: I like to provide prayer suggestions that you can also use to help you pray and understand God's best ways for you to proceed.

Here is that prayer: *God, I am looking for Your guidance and Your help. I want to ask You how I am supposed to proceed with this problem I am having. I am asking You to shed some light on this situation, to show me what I need to see, to help me understand the best ways to proceed and when to undertake those steps. Please speak to my heart clearly and concisely so that I know that You are the One guiding me. In Jesus' name. Amen*

God As Your Partner

When you make God your partner and you actually listen and follow through on the instructions He provides, you are much more likely to make good and smart decisions. You are going to know the right ways, even though at the time they may not seem like the right ways or the way may seem confusing to you. You may be feeling a bit confused as to the direction He is taking you but remember, **God knows best**. If you are still feeling confused and you really want to talk to Him about it, you can ask God to help you understand the direction He is taking you and you can ask God to help you understand the timelines involved.

Remember, when we say (as I do in all my books) that God wants that active relationship with you, it means that He wants you to know and to understand Him, His reasoning, His help and more. He invites you into an active relationship with Him for the purposes of showing you how much He loves you and how He is helping you.

I remember when I was looking to lose some weight a few years ago. I had never really made any efforts to lose weight in the past so I really wasn't sure of what I needed to do. The concepts of working out regularly and how to do so safely were not second-nature to me. Further, I used to eat anything I wanted without much regard for fat content, carb content, etc. My purpose for telling you this is because I wasn't aware of what I needed to do to lose that weight in the right ways and so when God guided me to eat more healthy foods and begin cardio workouts, I was honestly a bit taken aback. I had never given much thought to either but when I began to engage in both healthier eating and working out, I not only experienced weight loss and looking better but I also experienced greater mental health and greater energy levels, not to mention better sleeping habits.

Stop...And Consider

Another example of stop and pray about it is the following: I will never forget someone I know who had a property that they wanted to rent out and they were motivated to make it "move". They were so motivated that the first offer that came to them, they were jumping on it. I thought: "Hmm...maybe we should consider this offer a little more carefully and look at the givens."

When we looked closely at the deal being presented, we got to see that it was not a very good offer. You see, when people get the sense that you are motivated, they can sometimes try to take advantage of that. As such, we have to be very aware and consider things carefully instead of just jumping.

A lady I know was also in that situation. She had received an offer to join a new friend of hers on a luxury vacation and she seemed quite excited about it. She was downright jubilant and explained that she had never had such an exciting offer before. The luxury vacation included a direct flight, included all meals and drinks, all entertainment, port charges and maid services. It seemed like a great opportunity. I encouraged her to ask a few questions from this new friend of hers to get a greater sense of why he wanted to cover her expenses. Upon closer examination, she began to see that there were presentations that would be happening aboard and that these presentations were pressure tactics to get her to buy timeshare properties. She began to see that this "great" vacation offer was more of an exercise in coercion to get her to purchase something she would not have ultimately enjoyed, not to mention the fact that her new friend would be getting his ticket comped if he could "encourage" her to purchase one of the properties. That was going to be his kick-back.

> Considering opportunities carefully is an exercise in patience, in wisdom and in taking the time to understand when something is the right way to go versus the wrong way.

Considering opportunities carefully is an exercise in

patience, in wisdom and in taking the time to understand when something is the right way to go versus the wrong way.

Opportunities, people, etc. can come into your path and can seem great at first. Taking smart risks is about being knowledgeable and preparing properly for what could happen.

This applies to all areas of life but also heavily to you investors out there. There are wonderful investments out there that can do a great deal of good for your portfolio and your bottom line but it is buyer beware. Consider everything and ask the right questions. There will be things that people don't tell you but that you needed to know. The people involved have certain responsibilities to their buyers but sometimes those responsibilities don't go far enough and many likely won't go beyond that basic responsibility.

A couple of young ladies I knew didn't understand money, credit cards and lines of credit very well. They enjoyed shopping as much as many others do and they enjoyed being able to charge their credit cards for their purchases. What they were not paying attention to are the interest charges that can accrue as a result of not paying off the entire balance owed by a certain time. They figured (because their parents had done the same things all their lives and that was just how that family operated) that as long as they are paying off the minimum balance, that that would be enough. Not so. Not if you want to get further in life and not be sacked with a mountain of debt.

You see, the girls were looking only at the fact that they could buy whatever they wanted and wouldn't need to worry about making any of their full payments, which they figured was a good way of avoiding paying for now. They were not seeing how they were actually accumulating bad debt and getting themselves into a bad financial situation. Once they began to read the fine print, they began to discover that their thinking was faulty.

They began to consider more carefully if their purchases were really worth all that they were paying, in the end considering the high interest, etc.

3

Mortgages and Lines of Credit

Mortgages and lines of credit are also quite risky. Depending on the contract you have signed or are considering signing, you are promising the issuing financial institution that you are guaranteeing that you will make these payments at these points in time. You are not, at the time you are signing it or considering, thinking that something could happen to your income stream which could prevent you from making those payments. You are not, at the time of signing or considering it, thinking that something could happen and you might not be able to make those payments. You are taking a leap of faith - should you?

Here are my questions:

- Have you carefully thought this through?

- Why are you signing this contract?
- Is it necessary for you to sign this contract?
- Is it necessary for you to commit yourself to this deal or could there be a better one out there for you?
- Is this a wise move and have you read the contractual givens carefully?
- Why are you buying this property?
- Have you prayed about it?
- If you have prayed about it, what do you believe God is telling you about it?
- Does God say this is the right time to buy this property or to make this move?

We sometimes take nonsensical risks (risks that have not been calculated) and unfortunately, we will pay the price for them. Imagine if you have overextended yourself and you are unable to make those payments. The financial institution is not just going to let you off. They are not just going to forgive your now-inability to pay because you lost your job or some other unforeseen reason. They are going to charge you.

For many, if I were to ask them if they have a security cushion in case they can't make their payments, I'm not sure many would have a very good or solid answer. For many, if I were to ask them what are the penalties if you cannot make your payments, they wouldn't be able to answer that. And that's pretty risky because you are signing on the dotted line for something you are not sure you can undertake.

I am not trying to scare you. I am trying to make you aware of the potential pitfalls that exist when you sign on the dotted line without making informed decisions where you have considered the risk thoroughly. I am also trying to make you aware of the availability of praying about something to see if it really is the best opportunity or option for you. There may be other opportunities and options that are less risky, more beneficial and that ultimately give you a better return.

> It is when you are not informed that you will make your mistakes.

It is when you are not informed that you will make your mistakes. And those mistakes will be costly, I don't care who you are. In life, we are all in some way, shape or form (I assume) trying to get ahead. When we don't take the time to consider something that is so serious carefully, we are careening toward unpleasant, costly situations.

Prayer Suggestion: *God, I am considering entering into an important financial decision that will affect me, my family and more. I am asking for Your divine wisdom and guidance. Show me the way I should go. Show me how I am supposed to proceed with this so that I am doing Your will and in Your way and so that I am able to make the wisest financial decisions. Light the way for me, God, and show the best ways because I don't know or I am not sure. Also, please, make it clear to me that it is You who is guiding me and not the enemy misleading me. In Jesus' name. Amen*

Making God your partner in your decision-making process is always the right way to go.

When God Says No

Reader, I would like to impress upon you how important it is to not proceed when God indicates to you to not do something. All of the following are indications that this is not for you:

- general feeling of uneasiness
- general feeling that something doesn't feel quite right
- not having had your concerns met and your questions answered
- God seems to be saying no to you
- your conscience is bothering you about some part or all of the transaction

Do not ignore it when God tells you not to proceed. He

sees things you don't, He knows things you don't and He knows how to guide you away from something with feelings of uneasiness or uncertainty when something doesn't feel quite right. It may be difficult to walk away from something that seems right but that in the end, is not. Always trust your "gut feeling" which is also known as the Holy Spirit inside of you. He is always speaking - make sure you are listening.

4

Negotiate

Everything is negotiable in some form or other. If you are not negotiating, then you are not acting very wisely. Negotiating does not mean being belligerent, yelling, or being disrespectful. It means discussing so you can ensure that what you are signing for is the best deal.

When you don't negotiate, it is a way for the other party to have the impression that you don't really care, that you aren't willing to put in the time and the effort to discuss and to figure something out together or that you are not well-informed enough to care and that can signal to them that they can take advantage of you. Not negotiating says that you don't really care and that you are willing to, for one reason or another, accept anything the other party says. When you don't bother to negotiate, trust me when I say that the other party will walk away with a really good deal and it won't likely be so for you. So, in that frame of mind, negotiate appropriately.

Not sure how to. I have a suggested prayer for you for that too: *God, I know that negotiating is a really important thing to do. I know that negotiating is going to get me closer to a better deal and it communicates some important things to the other party. You are the best negotiator in the world because You have infinite knowledge and foresight. I am asking You to give me the tools, the opportunities and the words I need to negotiate in the best ways possible and I am asking You to show me when the right time is to enter into those negotiations. Give me the words, the appropriate intonation and the right ways to do this. In Jesus' name. Amen*

An Example

I recall very clearly when I was negotiating a real estate deal and the other party seemed to be on the same page as me. The other party was negotiating in good enough faith and I responded to her concerns, helping her to see the reality (and value) of the property. We were moving along nicely and as per the rules, I asked her follow-up questions to see how serious she was about the deal. We had been discussing the deal for at least a week when she turned around and notified that her dad is a realtor and that he would now be acting on her behalf. I was a bit taken aback by that and so didn't respond at first. Within an hour, her realtor dad called me and was belligerent. What he was trying to do was dominate the discussion and to dominate me. He was trying to intimidate me into giving his daughter a better deal and was actually lying about the rules to do so.

When you are in a negotiation, you lose 100% of the discussion (and your credibility) when you start to lie about facts. You lose the discussion and your credibility when you start to yell and you start to try to dominate the discussion. That's when the conversation ends (or, when the conversation should end). There is no place for yelling and being belligerent when you are negotiating and discussing a deal. If the person is being unreasonable and trying to dominate you, that means it's not the right deal for you.

In the right ways, you should negotiate. Appropriately and professionally.

In the right ways, you should negotiate. Appropriately and professionally. You should talk calmly but firmly to the other party but even before you do that, visualize and pray for the best results. I know many people who do that and they walk swiftly and beautifully into negotiations and they emerge the calm victor, making sure the discussion and the deal was the right one for them.

I recall one lady negotiating a lease deal and she was a very kind and calm operator. She discussed the terms, stated why the terms were as such and when a particular change needed to occur on the lease, she respectfully explained it. She ended up getting the exact lease she wanted for her client and doing so without breaking a sweat.

Negotiate the terms, the payments, the givens. All points should be negotiated and in every negotiation, there has to be some give and some take. Again, if there isn't, it's not the right deal for you.

People often assume that with financial institutions, we cannot give and take. They often erroneously assume that they just have to accept most of the terms a FI presents them with, save for some very minor details. This simply isn't true. I recall working with one FI and they presented me with much higher interest rates but didn't give me enough time to shop around and look for others. To add insult to injury, I had been dealing with the same person there for some time and without any forewarning or heads-up, the person in charge left for vacation smack in the middle of when my renewal was up. It was not a great conversation with the person's colleague that I had to deal with but it needed to get done and I did get an apology and a much more reasonable interest rate out of it.

Giving Yourself Time

As much as we expect organizations to give us sufficient

heads-ups on when something is due or when payment details need to be negotiated, many organizations don't and in the end, you stand to lose. As such, I suggest keeping track of your own deadlines, due dates and renewals. If you need to, approach them about your renewal, showing them that you are on the ball.

Give yourself time to look elsewhere if you don't like what you are receiving and give yourself time to understand and see where alternate possibilities lie.

When we give ourselves time, we benefit in all of the following ways:

✔ quietly and conscientiously consider all the givens
✔ take time to think things through
✔ have needed conversations with organizations
✔ talk to others (friends, family, colleagues) to see what their take is
✔ pray about the situation
✔ have time to really reflect on what you're doing and whether this is a good step
✔ find creative alternate solutions

It is often true that when we look for alternate (better) solutions, we end up finding them!

Negotiating also has to do with advocating for oneself and

ensuring that you are doing all that you can to ensure the best deal for yourself. Any deal is going to mean that you are going to have to live with the givens for a long time. As such, you want to be sure that you are getting the best deal possible and that it is something that you can actually live with. If you can't (if the deal is not realistic), it is going to be very difficult for you to live up to its expectations.

Negotiating does not need to be a bad word. Many people assume that it is but having a conversation where you are appropriately advocating for yourself does not need to be bad. Further, many people who are not very comfortable with confrontation believe that negotiating is synonymous with being difficult, with being unkind, or being rude. We can advocate for ourselves with kindness and pleasantly by speaking nicely and by simply pointing out what we would like to see in a contract that you are going to be subjected to.

Don't be afraid to appropriately advocate for yourself.

Don't Be Afraid

I want to make sure I make this clear, dear reader: don't be afraid to appropriately advocate for yourself and to state your points. Advocating appropriately means all of the following:

* speaking firmly but in a non-aggressive tone
* making your points thoroughly
* talking about why you deserve this
* mentioned how you have worked hard for this
* ensuring the person knows all the ways you have worked hard to make this happen
* letting the person know (gently) if any glitches were present that prevented you from doing what you needed to do
* letting the person know if things happened that were outside of your control and therefore, you cannot be held responsible for them (ex. a computer system failure happens and you were unable to complete the work in the time frame provided)

People will respect you more for doing so and if they don't, it's not the right place or person to be doing business with.

5

Make the Space

Life is busy. I get it. We all have many things to do and we all have many places to go, people to see, etc. I respect peoples busy schedules but you also have to **be mindful that you are making the space in your life to make those good & intelligently strategic decisions and most of the time, we need quiet time to make those good and strategic decisions.**

The best and most high-quality thought-processes and decisions come when we are alone, in the quiet and in our own space following prayer and meditation in silence.

The Holy Spirit is best able to speak to us when we

have prayed for His help and His guidance and when we are open to hearing from Him. Being open to hearing from Him means that we are asking Him questions and we are listening carefully and patiently to His input.

I remember very vividly when I was praying to be able to negotiate well in a particular business transaction. I was not sure how things were going to go or even if the person was going to be open to hearing my ideas, thoughts or input. In my quiet time, I prayed for God to open the door to make it the best possible interaction and to have the most positive outcomes. What ensued was tremendous. Never before had I had a positive interaction with the person with whom I was speaking but this time was different. In fact, he started the meeting by apologizing to me for his past actions and the way he had treated me in the past and let me know that he was open to a fruitful meeting and was willing to meet me halfway. This was not a particularly pleasant person from previous interactions and he was very much being very pleasant with me this time around. I did walk away from that meeting having gotten much more out of it than I would normally have.

One of my take-aways with this is: **if you ask God to help you out, He will. If you don't ask Him to help you out, He won't.**

Making the space means making the time in your life for thinking through and carefully considering a risk prior to taking it.

Making the space means making the time in your life for thinking through and carefully considering a risk prior to taking it. This could mean making sacrifices such as not going to a social outing, or not taking this opportunity or that one because it will take your time away from spending the time thinking, meditating and praying on your next steps.

Sacrifices

Simply put, you are not going to get away from making sacrifices for things that are important to you. Making sacrifices is required for anything you want to accomplish in life. Greatness does not happen without driving, striving and making sacrifices. For example, if you have a decision to make and you are considering it from various angles, you are not going to be able to do so by busily working on other things. The best way to make a wise and strategic, Holy Spirit-inspired decision is to take the time to pray about it and think things through, taking the time to meditate on what God is telling you to do. Decisions have many parts and pieces to them, as they also have repercussions no matter what you decide to do.

When we give it the quiet time and space that it needs, we are going to see the best quality results come through and we will flourish as a result.

Another point that is really important to mention is that when we sacrifice to make our goals come to fruition, that is a big signal to God and to people that we are willing to make time and space for this in our lives because we know that greatness does not come easy. It takes sacrifice.

Greatness does not come easy.

Sacrifice comes in many forms:

- Sacrifice of money
- Sacrifice of time
- Sacrifice of brain power
- Sacrifice of opportunity cost (of not doing something else in that time)

Because accomplishing anything worthwhile is going to

require sacrifice, we have to be sure that we are spending our time doing the right things. The "dead works" to be repented of are works performed by those who are "separated from the life of God" (Ephesians 4:18). These works may be religious in nature, but they are "dead" in that they cannot bring spiritual life.

So think carefully, pray frequently, select wisely and consider with all the givens because when you decide to undertake a route, you will be committing time, resources and much more to undertaking that.

Prepare

Further, when we pray for something, we have to prepare to receive it. If you are looking to land that new job, make space for it by driving by the company and claiming it as your new company. If you are looking to have another baby, prepare a baby's room and get the crib ready with all the things you are likely to need to make it a great baby's room. If you are looking to pay off your mortgage faster, consider getting tenants in the home and having them help pay down the amount you owe with their rent payments. If you are looking to have a better relationship with someone, take the time to make plans with them, to connect with them, to listen to them and to let them know that they should feel comfortable in coming to talk to you as you will be a trusted source for them. Lastly (but certainly not least), if you are looking to establish something new in your life, set aside some time each day whenever you can and work on visualizing its accomplishment or attainment.

When you prepare, you will be more ready when it manifests. When you don't prepare, you won't even know what to do when it does manifest and that won't be a good place to be. I will use the example of Karina here: Karina is an actress and had wanted a role in a Broadway play. She had prayed about it, visualized it, meditated on it and when the time came, the job opportunity came up. She was thrilled but she was not prepared. How do I mean that? She had not taken the time to prepare her audition tape, she had not memorized the lines or the song she was going to need to sing, she had not worked on how to best prepare and present her audition in light of the pandemic. Because she was not prepared, her audition did not go as well as she would have liked. The casting directors noticed this and while they appreciated her raw talent, they did let her know that she was not quite ready or right for the part. Karina was devastated. She had been waiting for this opportunity and it was now here, in front of her but because she hadn't been prepared and she did not make the space for it in her life by taking the time and doing what was necessary for her to be prepared, she did not do as well as she could have.

Reader, I tell you this not to scare you but to impress upon you how important it is to be ready and to do a great job at something by preparing for it and making space for it. We have to make space in our mind and in our physical space in order to be ready to conquer something when the time is right. You can consider this to be your call to get ready, prepare and make the space for whatever it is you are looking to accomplish.

God bless!

6 |

Smart Social Connections

We live in a social world. Connections and contacts matter. People need others and that is not likely to change. Therefore, whether you consider yourself to be a people person or not, you will need to make smart and strategic, authentic connections. You are going to need to network with the right people who are going to be able to help you to get to where you are looking to go. You are going to need to talk to people and to figure out the steps that are required to get to where God is guiding you to go. Authentic connections means that you are being yourself and not a "fake" version of yourself because you think it's what they want to see.

For example, when I was looking to get my manuscripts published and things with my publisher at the time were taking a lot of time, God was very clearly guiding me to learn the publishing landscape a little bit more deeply and to start learning how to format my manuscripts and learn to create, publish and distribute my own books. This was a definite shock for me because I knew, really, nothing much about how to create the actual book, format it and make it look good both on the inside and the outside. How did I get by? How did I learn what I had to do? I relied on conversations with people in the industry and with some more experience than me and I relied on videos that were posted from people who had been there, done that and could tell me about the systems that were currently available and their benefits and drawbacks. There were a few systems that were available and to my untrained eye, they all seemed fine but I knew that there would be differences in each that I didn't yet see or realize how important those small differences were. So what did I do? I prayed about it and I asked God to show me the best avenue to take, and the best system to use. He clearly guided me to one in particular that He made clear to me was the best one to use and guided my attention to the system's features menu which told me a little more about why God was guiding me to that one. Because I was still relatively new at this, I chose to go with the system God guided me to and fast forward several months and a very steep learning curve of understanding how to navigate the system and I am now fully confident I made the right choice. The current system I use allows for changes to be made quite easily, for the books to be properly displayed and available on the market, allows me to keep track of expenses and sales data and much more.

I took a risk but because I did my homework and prayed about it and went the way God was guiding me, the risk paid off and continues to work well today, for which I am very grateful because the system I use allows me to access all the information I need in one place.

Taking risks and sacrificing are not going to be easy things to do but when we look carefully, read everything, and rely on God's wisdom to help us, it can be made much much easier. Having God's guidance at my disposal in this decision-making process and in all others makes the task manageable and I have the King of Kings helping me through each step. So do you. Are you tapping into that?

Did I have many industry connections to help me and guide me in doing this? I did not. I had none but that didn't stop God from being able to bless me or you. He uses what we have and where we are to propel us forward and to help us accomplish what we need to and in doing so, helps us to help others. For example, there are many who need to hear that God desires a meaningful, personal relationship with each of us and that's why I spend time talking about that. There are also many who need to know how God speaks to us and what "follow Christ" actually means. (I know that when I was first starting out, I had 0 idea about what that actually meant). I also find it important to mention here that when I say important connections, that those can come in various ways. The connections I made were not face to face connections - they came in the form of pre-made videos and webinars that I found online from people much more familiar with the publishing industry and who were able to teach me a thing or two about the industry. There were also videos that showed me step-by-step how to use the publishing system, its provisions and limitations.

Connections can come from anywhere and can serve us very well. Ask God to bring you the connections you need and ask Him to open your eyes and give you the words you will need to communicate and to ask the probing questions that are required. And when He brings you those important connections, remember to treat the person well because not only do people in general enjoy being treated kindly, but it's the right thing to do to treat a person well, whether you are being helped by them or not.

What Goes Around....

I have to take a moment here to mention that what goes around does really come around. What you do unto another will come back to you in some way, shape or form. When you treat someone well, they appreciate it (whether they express that or not) and in turn, they too usually would like to do some nice things, maybe for you and maybe for someone else. You see, when you do something kind or nice for someone else, they appreciate it and they in turn may very well choose to do something kind for someone else. We shouldn't do kind things unto others to get a return but people are generally prompted and encouraged to do nice things for others when they too are treated well.

This ties in with my point of connecting with and learning from others. When we are learning from someone, know that they are gifting us. They are gifting us knowledge, help, advice, know-how and just to receive some guidance would be such a huge blessing to most. When this happens, the world becomes just a bit more of a better place to be. Kindness breeds kindness. Goodness breeds goodness. Taking it down to the tiniest example - when we do something nice for someone, like giving them a smile as we are passing them in a hall or in the street, generally, the person smiles back at us. They may very well return the kindness and society becomes just a little bit better.

So when someone takes time to help you, be grateful, acknowledge it in any way that you can and thank them for that. And if you can, pay it forward.

Asking God to Bring It To You

God knows the connections you need better than you do. He knows the landscape, the industry, the people you need to know, He knows what is necessary for you to move ahead and get ahead. Why not ask Him to bring you the connections you will need? Why not ask Him to place you exactly where you need and when to be there so that you benefit from the right person.

We can spend time "sucking up to" or chasing after a person because we may see them as our ticket to help. But they may not be. Ask God to help you with that. Ask Him to bring you the right person or the right people to help you.

I recall very vividly how at work, a woman was working diligently at getting close to the boss. She would follow her around, talk to her all the time, ask her questions and offer to do things for her. She was sucking up to her big time and she clearly wanted to be seen by the boss, trying to make herself known. The issue was that this boss was on her way to retirement and would not be able to do anything for this woman. Because she was near retirement (something she hadn't shared with anyone), she would no longer be in a position to help this woman out. Let me tell you how quickly the woman stopped spending time with her once she found out that she would no longer be in a position to help her. All the time she had spent following this woman around was wasted. Going back to my point: if this woman had spent some time praying and finding out where the right connections would be, maybe she would not have wasted her time and her resources on the wrong person.

Our time, friends, is limited. We have to make good decisions about how to spend our time and where to allocate our limited resources. We all have a "bucket list" if you will of things we would like to accomplish and we all have many things we would like to do in life. Because our time is limited, we don't have years to waste on the wrong thing - that's why

I say that asking God for His help in determining the right place to be, the right path to follow, the right avenues to take would be so important. If we don't do this, we will likely not be making the most of our time on earth and working strategically on accomplishing the right things.

God Knows All. God Sees All.

God knows all and He sees all. He knows where your time will best be spent. He knows who will be the right connection, with whom you would find favor and where you should invest your time. Don't be like the lady I used to work with and spend time on the connection you think you should be following. Things can be very deceiving - do not rely on your own understanding.

Here is a prayer that you may find helpful in getting you to God's guidance on this (remember, a prayer can be said out loud or in your mind, both are equally effective: *God, I need Your help. I am looking to get ahead in life and I need Your help and Your guidance in doing so. Show me the right path to take. Help me see the right way to go because I am not seeing it right now. Help me to do the right things and to find favor with the right people. Your word says that I am not to lean on my own understanding but that I am to rely on You. Well, here I am. I am relying on You and I am asking You to show me the right way, to make things happen for me in the right ways.*

In Jesus' name, I ask for Your direction, guidance, and open doors. Amen

Pay Attention...The Holy Spirit Will Be Speaking

Now that you have prayed, pay close attention to what God is saying to you. Pay close attention to new doors opening, new ways to get in and get ahead, new avenues. Now that you have prayed, God does His part in talking to you, in helping you and in guiding you. Pay close attention to what is happening around you now so that you can see where you are supposed to be going.

I make the point here again that prayer is a two-way conversation. This means that you speak and then you need to listen because God will be speaking as well. And this is a great blessing - the Creator of the Universe is speaking to you, helping you, imparting His wisdom onto you. How great is that! I know I would want to listen to that!

7

God-Strategy

There is a big difference between being dedicated and being strategically dedicated in God's ways.

Being dedicated means that you are committed to working hard at something you have chosen to take on. Being strategically dedicated means that you have prayed about what you are supposed to spend your time on, and you are dedicating your time, efforts and resources to that thing that God has led you to be dedicated to. When God directs you to be dedicated to something, it means that you will need to be all in to be successful at it. You cannot be dedicated to something and not be all in. When you are dedicated to work, you are very present, you put in 110%, you go above and beyond, you work consistently and strategically, you put in your best as often as possible.

When you are dedicated to your home life, you are very

present, you put in 100%, you go above and beyond for your family, you put in everything you can as often as possible. Any way you slice it, you will need to put in your all. You will need to put in the time, the effort and the work even when you don't feel like it, even when it's annoying, even when you feel tired, exhausted and just not in the mood. Wouldn't it be smart and strategic, therefore, to put in that much effort, dedication, time and energy into the right things that God has guided you to do?

Dead works are the works of our hands that we as humans think we should be undertaking without any input, or guidance from God. These are works of self righteousness, and they are appropriately called "dead" works because they lead to death (meaning, to nothing of value or significance). Twice the book of Proverbs says, "There is a way that seems right to a man, but its end is the way to death" (14:12; 16:25). We rely on work. We get significance from our work. We like a job that is well done. And well we should, because God created us to work. Yet all of our labors are useless, and thus dead, if they do not point to the worship of God.

And when we don't consult with or ask God where we are supposed to put our time, energy and resources then we are engaging in dead works, works that will not be fruitful and will not bring us what we think or hope that it will.

A lady I know is a great example of one who works to perform dead works. She received her Masters that God did not guide her to. She received a job offer for a high-paying job that God did not guide her to. She married a man that God did not guide her to. In her work, she does not use her Masters degree (not does her compensation match up with what a professional with a Masters degree should be getting), her job brings her zero fulfillment and she does not enjoy what she is doing, and the man that she married consistently leads her away from God, instead of toward Him. All of her works are dead works and they are not and will not lead to the abundance and success she thinks they will lead to.

Ask yourself this question: are you engaging in dead works? Are you taking on unintelligent risks that you don't need to be engaging in? Are you spending your time, energy and resources on things that God has not guided you to and there-fore, are not going to yield what you think they will yield?

Take a few moments and use the space provided here to reflect on these questions:

Everything Is A Risk

Truthfully, everything is a risk. Every endeavor you take on is a risk. When you step out of bed in the morning, you are taking risks. When you choose to go to work, you are taking a risk. When you drive your car, you are taking a risk. When you engage in discussions with colleagues and bosses, you are taking a risk. When you spend time with family and friends, you are taking a risk.

What are you risking? Your time, energy and resources. With time being the most valuable resource we have. So wouldn't it make sense to use your resource in the best ways possible? When we engage in dead works, we are wasting our most valuable resource and many other resources as well. Going back to the example of the lady I know engaged in dead works, she is wasting her time, her money, her energy, her efforts, etc. Being one who prays for others, I have gently let her know that I don't think she is in the right place and space. I know that she takes to heart what I am saying and that this concept has stuck with her but when we realize that things may not be right, we have to turn our attention to God and get His guidance. That is something she has not chosen to do.

So until you do that, you will be engaging in dead works. You will be toiling in vain.

Going back to my point, everything is a risk. Why not take the smartest risks possible and put your best into what God is guiding you to do. After all, He created you and He knows you best so He knows what skills, competencies and abilities He has put in you and where you are supposed to be channeling those.

8

Your Most Authentic Self & Mitigating Risk

There is lots of talk these days about being your most authentic self. And I get that. People should be recognizing and celebrating their most authentic selves and **your most authentic self is who God says you are.**

We are all on a journey of discovery and that discovery is best done with a map that allows us to see where He is leading and guiding you to be. For example, Dan was leading his life in one way and was an accountant working at a large accounting firm, working hard day in and day out and dating a woman whom he had no intention of marrying. He was stringing her along. Everything changed when Dan made a life-changing prayer and asked God to reveal to him where He wanted him to be and what He wanted him to do. Dan had never previously felt connected to any part of his life - he almost felt like he was living someone else's life. A couple of realizations hit Dan very hard when he realized that he was not living his most authentic life: he realized that he had no interest in working for this company and that his accounting skills could be better suited elsewhere and he realized that he was not being fair to this woman he was dating because he had no intentions of making things forward with her. When he prayed again, he asked God to open the right doors for him and to close the wrong ones. Almost immediately, Dan was pink-slipped from the company he had been working for and received a very generous compensation package and then decided that he wanted to go and work for the same accounting firm his dad had worked for for over 35 years. His dad had a strong legacy there and upon applying, Dan was hired immediately, even though they hadn't advertised any openings. He then very kindly and gently ended things with the woman he had been seeing, letting her know that this didn't feel entirely right and that he wished for her to find her God-blessed happiness. She too admitted that things didn't feel right with him and thanked him for being honest and letting her go. With his decision to follow God's best for him, Dan completely turned his life around and things really began to fall into place.

Dan felt tremendously grateful that he could follow God and be happier than he thought he could be. Slowly, he began to rise in the ranks at the company, just like his dad had done years prior and created a nice retirement fund for himself. Through this company, he got to know a co-worker with whom he clicked tremendously and he made the choice to ask her out. She agreed. They are in love today and committed to each other. Also, because Dan was working for the same company as his dad, they began to talk more, share more information and trade tips and best practices, and they began a weekly Sunday brunch outing where they could talk, connect and enjoy accounting trade talk. This one decision to change this part of his life meant wonderful changes for Dan and a much closer relationship with his dad.

When we live our most authentic life in Christ, we are taken on some changes and we will experience shifts (sometimes huge shifts) in our lives, all meant to make you a better person and happier, because it's God's will for you. He knows what will make you the happiest and feel the most fulfilled.

All of the following examples are of people who have gone from dead works to a meaningful, active relationship with God where they are living their most authentic, best life. Take a look.

When you make changes in your life, expect that some people will be along for the ride while others will have a stop and get off. And that's ok. Know that you are spending time, effort, and energy on the people who are meant to be there.

I would also like to note that all of the people who are mentioned here deserve to be applauded for the changes they have made in their lives, to live their most authentic life in Christ. Each took steps to transform themselves and live their worth in Christ. Remember that when you make such changes, some people will remain in your life and others will not. And that's ok. You should congratulate yourself for having had the courage to make a positive, life-affirming change in your life and to be sure that you are treating yourself as well as possible.

Name	Dead works	Change	Most authentic life

| Mark | Mark had 0 relationship with God and he engaged in illegal acts. He would regularly take drugs and sell them. | Mark felt the call of God and began going to rehab in his hometown of Colorado. When he began to realize that while off the drugs, he was able to think better and that he began to feel better, he realized that he did not want to continue with his previous way of life. | Mark began living a more authentic life of being in communion with God. In this new relationship, Mark began to attend church, and felt the call of God to be a pastor of a youth church. Today, he remains sober (5 years sober in fact) and he is working on getting his next educational degree that he feels strongly that God has led him to. |

Julie

Julie was married to George, a man who used to hit her. Because Julie's upbringing said that she did not deserve better (she had watched her father hit her mother) she felt that this was normal enough and did not want to do anything about it until the day her husband hit her so hard that she lost hearing in one ear.

Julie's friend invited her to church one day and Julie went, not telling her husband where she was going.

At church, Julie heard the messages of Christ's love for her and for all. She began to weep realizing that not once had she ever felt any love from George. When she spoke to the pastor in confidence, she led him know of her home situation, to

Julie began an active relationship with the church, helping to solidify her worth in her mind and helping George get the help he needed for his anger. Julie was taking a very big risk in her life, one that God had not called her to, and so she chose to dedicate her time to the church (she got a full time job there as a secretary, which she loved), helped George get which the pastor said that she does not need to accept that and provided her with some options.

into a treatment program and chose to end the marriage (something she felt strongly that God was calling her to do).

Raphael

Raphael was a very unkind man. He lied, cheated, took advantage of others in business. Raphael had a lot of anger inside and 0 respect for people, which his family and co-workers did not appreciate.

When Raphael's mother passed away, it was a big wake-up call for him. His mother ardently prayed for him and she would let him know that she did not raise him to be an unkind and dishonest man. He listened to her talk like that for years but nothing changed. Until her death. He finally realized that she was not there anymore to speak

Months after her death, Raphael yearned for his mother's love and attention. Her words resonated in his mind and he knew that she had not raised him that way. His absent father was that way and that was one of the reasons their marriage failed. Raphael began to slowly realize that despite loathing his absent father, he had become just like him. He her words of wisdom to him and that shook him. knew that he needed to change and that he needed to be better. This awakening was part of the catalyst that caused him to change.

Winnie

Winnie was a kind young woman who always wanted to do good unto others. Others, however, erroneously took Winnie's kindness as a sign of weakness and they took advantage of Winnie in life, in work, in personal relationships and more. Winnie realized that this was not the way she wanted to live her life.

Winnie began to see a Christian counselor to talk about how others would treat her in life. The poor way she was being treated brought her down a lot and she didn't enjoy it at all.

The counselor suggested to Winnie that it was time to stand up for herself and to communicate her worth to others. She also suggested that if people

Winnie made some great changes in her life and let some "friendships" go. She saw that not all in her life saw her worth and that she should only keep those in her life that valued her and treated her the way that she deserved.

Even though Winnie had to let some people go, she knew that she was doing the right things for herself and in her life could not accept her worth, that they didn't need to be in her life.

that she was asserting her worth to people.

Jason

Jason's fiance left him and broke his heart. She left him just prior to their wedding day. He felt lost and wasn't sure what to do.

Jason was raised a Christian and so, in his lost and confused state, he began to search the Bible and began listening to sermons. He began to learn again about the love of God and how there is a person meant for us but that the One to bring us that person is God.

Jason realized that he had undergone a very wrong search for the right woman. He had never prayed to God about who the right person would be and so he began to feel more and more convinced that his fiance leaving him was a blessing.

Jason decided to begin praying for his right woman and he made the choice to begin pursuing the ave-

nues and out-
lets that God
was guiding
him to.

Mack

Mack spent over 35 years working for a company where he felt undervalued, underpaid, and his boss and co-workers did not respect him. At the end of each work day, Mack felt that he had no value. He cried out to God for help and for God's guidance.

Mack knew things had to change because he felt so awful inside. He felt like he needed help in getting out of this situation and to feeling valued.

Mack began to read the Bible and the book of Proverbs really began to speak to him. He felt that the wisdom there could benefit his life tremendously, if he put its practices into play.

Mack tendered his resignation to the company as he felt guided to do. He then began working at a new company doing the same thing and putting in the same effort. At this new company, Mack's skills were quickly noticed and he rised very quickly through the ranks. His work was not only acknowledged but it was revered. He felt valued and cared for, which is what he was look-ing for, in addition to being paid a lot more.

Making changes is not easy but when you spend time taking on and doing good works and things God calls worth-while, be confident that you are spending your time in the best possible ways. You would then be taking a very smart risk and doing things the way God meant for you to do them.

When you do things the way God intends, you will move forward in the right way. You will move forward in God's timing, a very important concept. More on that in the next chapter.

Congratulate Yourself...It IS A Little Win

Remember to congratulate yourself for not only calling out to God and seeking His way and His best for you but also, for taking the time to actually do what He tells you to do. I talk about little wins in my videos and other books (as well as this one) and you can certainly consider this a little win! (You can actually consider it a big win, but that's up to you).

9

Timing

Timing is very important. There is a time to get things done and there is a time to stay quiet in quiet, meditative contemplation. We may want God to do things in our time frame because that's just when we want it but we also need to be mindful that your "now" may not be the best time and God knows that.

Why might it not be the best time? All of the following reasons can apply:

- You may not get the full fruits of your labor if it happens now
- There may be a connection that we need in order for something to move forward and that connection has not been set up yet
- There may be something we need to learn prior to the blessing happening

- There may be someone whose heart God has to turn in order to make the blessing happen
- There may be things we need to learn in the meantime while this is all being done
- God may be trying to teach you patience in the midst of all of this

We Are Human

As humans, we want all good things now. We have to recognize, though, that it may not be the best time for something and that we may need to wait for something to be at its best, for God to line things up for us properly, or for us to learn and be humbled before the thing happens.

When we say timing has to be right, we can pray to ask God when that timing would be right. God loves to communicate with us and loves to tell us things about our goals, including its details, timeline and more.

Going Ahead of God

Sometimes, we don't listen when God doesn't make something happen when we want it to and so we move ahead of Him. This can lead to a disastrous situation and with disastrous consequences. Here is an example: Dickie wanted to be married and quickly so. He had met a lovely woman named Sherrie and he felt that this "is it"! Dickie was ready to move ahead and propose, so he did. He did not ask God, he didn't even ask any friends or family. He just moved ahead and asked Sherrie to marry him. She accepted and they were married quickly. And then....disaster. Because Dickie moved so quickly into marrying Sherrie, and without asking all the right questions, he realized that their definitions of marriage were wildly different. Sherrie believed in open marriages and in experimenting while Dickie was all about the traditional marriage, the same kind his parents had had. When they discussed this, Dickie expressed his views but Sherrie was having none of it. In fact, because she had never really learned to compromise on anything she felt thoroughly offended by what Dickie expressed and she told Dickie that if he didn't want an open marriage, that he would be left behind. Sherrie then proceeded to begin to entertain other men in their home, disrespecting Dickie's wishes and disrespecting Dickie.

To make matters worse, because Dickie had not properly prepared for the marriage in terms of protecting himself, he realized that by divorcing Sherrie, he would lose out on much. He felt stuck and unsure of what to do. Sherrie was not the person he thought she was and now, he was stuck.

> God is able to see and know all that is right and best for us.
> He is able to guide us away from challenges and difficulties.

See, God is able to see and know all that is right and best for us. He is able to guide us away from challenges and difficulties that we were never meant to have and He wants to be able to keep us safe from unnecessary problems. Before we leap into something, we need to check it with God. We need to ask all of the following:

- Is this the best thing for me?
- Is this Your best for me?
- Is now the time that I am supposed to be undertaking this move?
- What else do I need to know about this move that I cannot see right now?
- What other details can you tell me about what to do with this?
- This person/company/situation seems very beneficial to my human mind and eye. Is it, God?
- What are the drawbacks (if any) of this situation?

Setting Things Up

One of the things God uses that time for is to set things up properly for you. That means that He is aligning the good breaks, the right people to come into your path, the right setup, etc. We have to remember that the God of the Bible wastes nothing. He uses time very efficiently and effectively, ensuring that He always does His part in setting things up right for us.

So, knowing that, use that waiting time to be specific in your ask. Outline for God what you would like and how you would like it. Outline the particular givens, and think about it from all angles. Remember that if you don't ask for a particular detail, you are not likely to receive it so use that time wisely and be wary of what you are asking for.

Also, being grateful and expressing that gratitude ahead of time (even during the waiting time) would also be super and a good use of your time.

Reality Check

Life can be challenging. We all have things we are trying to do, to accomplish, to succeed at and good things take time. Great things take lots of time. This is why in this chapter, we are going to take a little reality check for a moment and we are going to explore great things happening.

We all have the skills and abilities to do great things. We all have talents, abilities, dreams and goals that we wish to see fulfilled but life is also challenging (sometimes very challenging) and if we don't take the time to work hard and respond to the spiritual needs, then that means that we are not putting in all that is required.

Some people come to my manifest coaching one-on-ones and they let me know the challenges they are facing. To that, I often say "Good!" I don't say that to be mean or hurtful but I say it because it means that they are on route and that the challenge is there because they are progressing and moving forward. If they were not progressing, then the challenge wouldn't exist. To illustrate what I mean, I will take the example of a husband-and-wife couple who are trying for their first. Let's say that they are experiencing some challenges but that they are working through them. The fact that they are working through them (i.e., going to appointments, doing medical tests, having those important conversations, etc.) are all steps toward accomplishing their goal of getting pregnant. On the flip side, they could not be having those conversations. They could not be attending those medical appointments and they could not be taking the necessary steps; that would mean that they are no further ahead in their process.

Life can definitely be challenging but we also have to remember that those challenges make the acquisition of the goal that much more meaningful and that much more special. How much do you appreciate having your name on title on a property, even though you may have a mortgage and you have to work hard to pay it off? How much do you appreciate the baby you had to go through fertility treatments to conceive? How much do you appreciate the fine dinner out when you had to work a month worth of overtime to be able to afford it?

It Won't Be Easy

If you are going into anything thinking it is going to be easy and there won't be much risk involved, I urge you to reconsider. Everything has risk attached, whether we see it right away or not. When we don't see the risk right away, we have to remember that we are just not seeing it with the naked eye.

What are some ways you can find out the risk involved with something? Try all of the following:

- ask people who have been there and done that
- read up on the industry and the situation
- ask for information meetings from people who work in the industry and know about it
- visit the place or the space before your appointed time to be there and check out the milieu
- if you are going to deal with a lot of paperwork, ask for the papers ahead of time to read all that is involved
- if you have an opportunity, dialogue with the people you will be working with and try to find meaningful connections with them so that you can have a really good starting-off point

When you are around people and you are presented with something to sign, people don't usually take the time to read it and consider it carefully because they are very conscious that there are people waiting on them, waiting for them to sign the papers. This can be very nerve-wracking and not at all conducive to taking your time and considering the clauses from all angles. There is nothing wrong with asking for the papers to be sent to you ahead of time so that you can take the time to consider everything carefully and to read through everything, noting your rights and responsibilities.

They Will Assume You Read Everything

Further to my point just above, know that the other party is going to assume that you read everything and that you are in the know about everything. If you do not know your responsibilities, your lack of knowledge will be held against you (along with pertaining and relevant fees). So do yourself a favor and know your stuff. Be prepared. Ask the right clarification questions. And make sure that when you do, you are getting clear answers.

Get It In Writing

Something that I use to make my life much easier is to get things (especially things with much detail) in writing. When I get it in writing, I can really look at it carefully and consider it from all angles. This may annoy some people who don't feel like writing it out but too bad. You are signing for something and/or accepting something - you need to know what you are getting yourself into.

Further, you want to make sure that you can refer back to the written information when you need to. With time, memories get fuzzy, we can forget details, and we can forget that we agreed to things. Getting it in writing means that you can refer back to it and you can refer them back to it as well. I recall very vividly when I was discussing a mortgage renewal with a FI (financial institution) and they had guaranteed me a certain rate. I got it in writing because months later, they were refusing to give me that rate and wanted to stick me with a much higher one). I was able to pull out the original document where they had promised me the lower rate and after a bit of discussion, they honored what they had said. If I hadn't gotten it in writing, I seriously doubt that I would have walked away successfully.

Clarify, Clarify, Clarify

Before you sign on the dotted line, clarify all points. If there is something you are not sure about or the wording does not make sense, clarify it. If the other party does not want to clarify it or you are still unclear about it, do not move forward. I will provide this example of this point: I will never forget a lease offer we received for a residential lease. The other party seemed to be offering all the things we asked for and they seemed to be amenable to any changes we wanted. Sounded great. But wait: I read a clause in one of the Schedules that didn't seem to make any sense. The wording was very tricky and strange and very convoluted. When I took my time and asked about it, the agent's response was just as convoluted. I realized that the clause that they were asking us to sign was basically saying that we had no right on a certain jurisdiction if the other party performed something specific - which made no sense.

Readers, I hope that I have impressed upon you the importance of reading things carefully, meditating on the givens and to making sure you know and are fully aware of what you are signing up for. There is also nothing wrong with asking questions and to asserting yourself so that you make sure that you are standing up for yourself.

Sharp Leadership When The Stakes Are High (Your 5 Step Guide)

Sharp leadership is absolutely imperative when the stakes are high and when risk is involved because everything has repercussions. Here is your 5 step guide to ensuring that you are displaying that sharp leadership during meetings, negotiations, discussions and more.

1. Be alert
2. Be the most prepared guy (or gal) in the room
3. Watch and learn quickly
4. Communicate in a powerful way
5. Create a risk-smart community around you

Be Alert

This is vital. You always have to be "on" and alert in leadership contexts. That means that you are listening carefully, looking around, absorbing all that is being said and not said (non-verbal communication is very important) and you have to make sure that you are listening and understanding other peoples positions and stances.

Sharp leaders who understand risk are ones who do not crumble under pressure and know how to keep it cool at all times, even if they are not feeling so cool on the inside. Smart leaders who understand risk and reward know that if you start panicking, you are already losing the game. And really, if you keep your cool and you stay alert to what is going on, you are not likely to be on the losing side. Negotiations can be intense but by staying alert and keeping your cool, you will come out the victor.

Be the Most Prepared Guy (or Gal) In the Room

Knowing who everyone is, their roles and functions, what they are bringing to the table in terms of input and influence, knowing how to navigate and get what you want from each person are all extremely important. You need to know the players and you need to know what is at stake and what you are negotiating for to make the deal the most favorable for you and your colleagues.

Destiny does not make appointments. We have to be ready

and we have to be prepared. When you are prepared and you know your stuff, you come in confident, equipped, ready and powerfully. Take the example of a person who is about to enter a business meeting and has to present. If they do not have their presentation down pat, they have not practiced and are not extremely well-versed in all that they will be saying, if they are not prepared to speak with conviction and with great dynamo, then how strong will that presentation be?

Conversely, how much more powerful would that presentation be if the person is thoroughly prepared, knows their stuff and is ready to knock any question out of the ballpark! Being the most prepared commands respect. Showing up early is also a sign that you are prepared and that you are ready to take the room.

Watch and Learn Quickly

We learn by watching others and by carefully analyzing what they are doing, how they are doing it and getting a sense of why they are doing what they are doing. When we learn to watch others, we pick up a lot of information about them, the contexts that surround them and their motivations (what drives them). One who learns quickly how to use that information to their advantage is a sharp leader indeed.

When you sit back and watch, you also begin the process of planning your next strategic move. You know your overall strategy and you can tailor your next move or do things outside of the order that you originally thought. And that's ok - that is called rolling with it. What is important is that you learned to get your points across and negotiate for your favor by applying your points in the right way and the right context.

Frankly, everyone has to learn the power and the ways of sharp leadership. It is a skill that is learned and those who learn it quickly and apply it steadily will be the victors and the ones who benefit. Those who don't learn it will flounder and will allow others to be the victors. Which side of the fence do you want to be on?

Select Communicate Is Powerful

Strategic communication is powerful and the ways that we choose to communicate are also very powerful. Context, tone, poise, timing and manner are very important and signal our intentions. We can be firm and direct while not being "jerk-like".

When we communicate firmly and decisively with others, it is vital to own what we are saying and to be and to project confidence when you are saying it. The right message said without authority, conviction and purpose can and will fall very flat.

The fact is, when we over-communicate and we say too

much, the other person stops listening. When you have made your point, please stop making it. Saying it once, with conviction, is the most powerful. Trust me, the other person heard it. Now it is a matter of them processing it and realizing you meant it and you are not going to waste your breath any further. It is also a way of you indicating that you are respecting your own point and that you are not going to keep making the same points again and again. That is power.

Create A Risk-Smart Community Around You

We are social beings (as I said earlier in the book) and the community and the people with whom we surround ourselves are tremendously important. The people around us rub off on us whether we like it or not and they do have a great impact on our thoughts, our actions, our temperament, our outlook and more. This is why we always need to try to surround ourselves with the smartest, strongest and best. You will learn from them and they (trust me!) will also be learning from you. If they are sharp, they will pick up tips and strategies from you too.

Bear in mind that when you associate with the wrong kind of people, you are setting yourself up for failure because bad company corrupts good character. If you do not have strong people with great examples in front of you or around you, then find examples you would admire online, in videos, on social media, etc. Even that will go a long way toward helping you become a stronger, more goal-oriented person and will help you strive for higher and better.

In the movie Coach Carter, we see how young basketball players have less than exemplary people around them. They are people who are academically low-achieving and they are people who have very low expectations set for them (and they were on their way to meeting those low expectations). Enter Coach Carter. This coach put a tremendous fire in them and helped them to rise to the occasion that they needed to aspire to. The coach met with tremendous resistance and was not initially viewed very favorably (with some students and even parents and guardians getting a bit physical with him) but nevertheless, the coach maintained his strong stance and transformed those players academically, mentally, socially, and in every way. Even an example from a movie like that can take a person a very long way.

God is Strategy

A very important point I find imperative to make at this point in the book is that many people do not realize that God is strategic. God is the smartest mind that has ever existed and as such, He knows exactly what He is doing and allowing at all times.

One may then say that when we spend that quiet time with

God, we will learn from Him and we will become wiser and smarter. WE ABSOLUTELY WILL! This is why the Book of Proverbs is so full of wisdom - it is God-inspired wisdom and you cannot get better than that.

When you pray, meditate, visualize, and spend time alone with God, know that you are reaping the benefits from the greatest mind that has ever existed. It is really important to note that God's wisdom exists for all of us and we need to be mindful and grateful for that.

Here is a suggested prayer to help you to tap into that wisdom: *God, I know that You are the all-knowing, all-wise, and that You are everywhere all the time. I am grateful that You have provided me with access to Your wisdom and to Your greatness through prayers, meditation, visualization and more. I am asking You to provide me with Your great wisdom. I am asking You to provide me with Your amazing knowledge about all of the situations I am currently dealing with and show me Your ways to handle them as intelligently and as strategically as possible. I am so grateful for You, God, and I wish to know You more intimately and more deeply. In Jesus' name. Amen*

Working On It

I would also like to add a note here that if you are not yet that sharp leader who is able to expertly read the room and proceed in a very strategic way, do not beat yourself up over it. As long as you are willing to be open to learning, to understanding, to growing, to knowing the better ways and being open to it all, then you are already well on your way to becoming a world-class leader.

Jesus (God) selected His apostles and followers from ordinary men. These were men who were average Joes (if you will) but what He did with them (how He transformed them and showed them God's amazing glory and miracles) was what was so astounding about the situations. It is amazing how God selected such ordinary people to follow Him but God also knows that ordinary men can and do have extraordinary abilities in them and can do some amazing things.

Before I close out this chapter, I want to share the following image with you. From this image, I hope you will see God's incredible love for the man in the image and His affection for him. I also hope you will see God's joy, care, kindness, affection, collegiality, and more. This is how God is all the time and when you come to Him to learn, to get better, to grow and to improve, He will always lovingly be there for you! I have provided some space below the image intended to give you some space to write down your thoughts and impressions on the picture and to jot down any ways you believe you would like to improve.

This section is all about forgiving yourself if you have made a move or a decision that ended up being unwise. If you did not make the right decision about something, whether you prayed about it or not, you have to get to a point where you forgive yourself and you move forward, past the error.

As long as you:
* learn from it
* see where you went wrong
* realize that you didn't pray about it as you needed to
* realize how you need to do it differently next time
* see the benefits of what I am talking about in this book
* commit to making the necessary changes and to doing it the right way next time

If you commit to making the changes needed and to doing it the right way next time, then you have learned from your mistake and you are ready to move forward. It is so important, dear reader, to learn and to grow and to not make the same mistakes again. If we don't do this the right way, we will face the hardships again and life is hard enough as it is. Don't make the same mistakes again and make sure that you check in with God and let the Holy Spirit speak to you properly, paying attention to all the advice He gives you and following His ways and His timing.

God bless!

I have provided some extra space here for the purposes of a reflection. Reflect on what I have said here and on your own next steps, thinking about how you can do better next time. Half the battle is learning and we have all made unfortunate mistakes that we have paid for. The best next steps is to try to mitigate those errors by asking God how.

FORGIVING YOURSELF

FORGIVING YOURSELF

FORGIVING YOURSELF

CHRISTINE TOPJIAN is an educator, author, writer, manifestation consultant and producer-performer. She has more than 17 years of experience in teaching online and face to face, and in growing businesses. She has worked in residential real estate for the past 15 years and in property management. She continues to grow her repertoire of books published and people reached by her videos, articles and in growing her social media following. She has written articles for the ACTRA Performer's Magazine, the Armenian Missionaries Association of America, and for the Markham Review. Her articles will next be appearing in Faith Today Magazine and their website version.

She is a graduate of Christian Leadership University in the States, Canisius College in Buffalo and Ryerson University in Toronto.

Her website is www.DrChristineTopjian.com.